Nightscapes

poetry from the depths

by **E.M. Welcher**

Nightscapes

poetry from the depths

by E.M. Welcher

The main street of the City was pure gold, translucent as glass. But there was no sign of a Temple, for the Lord God—the Sovereign-Strong—and the Lamb are the Temple. The City doesn't need sun or moon for light. God's Glory is its light, the Lamb its lamp! The nations will walk in its light and earth's kings bring in their splendor. Its gates will never be shut by day, and there won't be any night. They'll bring the glory and honor of the nations into the City. Nothing dirty or defiled will get into the City, and no one who defiles or deceives. Only those whose names are written in the Lamb's Book of Life will get in.

Eugene Peterson,
The Message,
Rev. 21:21-27

Table of Contents

WILL YOU STILL LOVE ME?

I have grown long in the tooth.

Hair sprouting

Everywhere.

I cannot get my meat rare enough.

I arise before dawn to go on the hunt.

Leave you in the den slumbering.

I smell my way home, blood on my hands.

Truck empty.

Stomach full.

Did I forget my gun?

Did I leave my kill in the forest?

I am a lifelong sleepwalker,

Assuring you it's not odd

To find me curled up at the foot of your bed,

Sullied, bare feet,

Rouged lips,

Wine, I surmise.

You nod.

Love means believing one another's lies.

It was only you, only ever you.

Your scent fills my nostrils.

I tracked you night after night.

I had eyes only for your tracks.

I want to hibernate with you.

And rise from the grave

Every Spring.

We'd stay up all night with our friends

And howl at the same full moon.

You are my Moon Goddess.

When we were human, love meant never leaving.

Will you love me enough

To place silver bullet in chamber

And pull the trigger?

Or live your life as my master? Can you tame a
monster?

What will the neighbors think about all their missing
chickens?

Who will cut the grass and take out the trash?

Will I dwell in the woods outside our house, your mate
for life?
If I am spotted, and I won't be, but if I am,
Will fear cloud the fact
That I have a man's eyes?

TANGLED

Tangled up in Dogwood Branches,

Hair, limb, & happenstances,

Soft summertime kisses.

We were kids, back then.

I became We.

Love & geography,

Religion & circumstances,

Tangled up in Dogwood Branches.

Tangled limbs, bed sheets, second chances.

Soft Summertime Kisses.

Hospitals.

Tears & People,

The feeble.

Tangled & Mangled.

Kissing dreams goodbye,

Kissing you goodbye.

Soft Summertime Kisses.

Tears & people.

Church & steeple.

Hope & mourning,

Mingled, tangled, mangled.

Dogwood coffin,

I sit on her stump often.

Where we used to get tangled,

Hair, heart, limb, and bramble.

Heart rattle...heart tattle.

I remember,

Soft Summertime Kisses.

Old man, frayed brown trousers.

World weary face, medicinal powders.

Empty mailbox.

Wall lined with pictures,

Of dead people.

I've been retired longer than you lived.

But I remember when we climbed high,

Memories, stories, limb & heart tangled,

High in Dogwood Branches,

Happenstances, Circumstances, and Second Chances.

And Soft Summertime Kisses.

I don't know what to do without you,

But Soft Kisses,

In The Summertime,

Of My Life,

Carry me through.

NAPOLEON

One Leg,
Outside The Covers.
Over The Covers.
Over You.
I Conquered The World,
With One Leg.

Sneak attack.

You let your guard down,

Closed your eyes,

Escaped to the land of Nod.

So you thought.

All is fair,

In Love & War.

Pretense: to the Loo.

But Alas!

You fool!

I'm turning the thermostat

down, down, down,

downtown,

to 32.

I return to bed,

Much relieved.

I crank the ceiling fan,

higher, higher, higher.

I marshal my artillery,
Advance out of my
1/16 of territory,
On the edge of eternity,
Into the land of Nod.

I pillage the comforter,
Yes, I take the grand prize first.
I take the sheets, I take all.
Nothing quenches my thirst,
I. Take. All.
Even your precious throw pillows.

I fortify my 1/16th.
Chateau La Couverture.

I bide my time.
Old Man Winter,
Will remind you of
My better qualities.
You'll remember,
I'm flesh and blood,
Warm as life,

Warm like friendship,
Before the war.

You'll come crawling back,
To my side,

Just to stay warm.

SURROUNDED BY BOOKS

It would have been,

Perfect, you know.

Me, a Pastor,

With a Church Building,

Surrounded by Books.

You, a School Teacher

With a School House

Surrounded by Books.

Us, a family,

Raising Children

In A Home,

Surrounded by Books.

NOTHING NEW

The Preacher Said,
"There's nothing new..."
My people enslaved you
For hick chew.
It's all about us,
Never you.
Nothing New.

My people,
Will always love you,
For what you can do,
Not for how God made you.
It's always about us,
Never you.
Nothing New.

You can't breathe,
And we can't see.
We won't look,
If it's not about us.
It is imperative

We star in the narrative.
It's ever about us,
Never you.
Nothing New.

We're Nowhere.
Nowhere a'tall.
Nowhereville USA.
Where the blood flows,
At the gas station,
In direct relation,
To the conservation,
Of our White imagination.

It isn't a Plague,
If it's Preventable.
He's not a Tragedy,
He's a Man,
He's not a teaching Moment,
He's a man.
Loved by God,
Made by His hand.
Nothing New.

FIVE YEARS

Five Years Ago
The Father gave you away.
Two Years Ago,
The Father took you away.
You're still dear
To Me.
You took away my fear,
That I was unlovable
When you said, "I Do."
I Do.

In Sickness.
In Health.
Dissolution of Self.
Reveling in self-forgetfulness,
'til I forgot the pain.
What I wouldn't give,
To kiss your bald head again.
Let's make a deal...

Two Long Years,

Your clothes
Neatly folded in your dresser,
Your Wedding dress hangs in the Closet,
For good measure.
I just keep the door closed.
Keep the door closed.

But Anger knocks,
And Pain knocks,
And Bitterness knocks,
And Guilt Knocks,
And it's all burning in my gut.
Gut Rot. Gut Knot.
Tied The Knot.
Forget Not.
And this door ain't what it used to be.
Hunny Bunny.
It's gunna take me out,
Before it takes out the Damned Cancer.

So...
I try to smile,
At least once a day,

For you.

You took my hand,
And let me put a Ring
On yours.
I am yours.
I buried mine,
With you,
Down in steamy St. Louis.
Bury me,
Bury Me With You.

I sit amongst the Graves,
Dreaming of Resurrection Day,
Maybe You'll place your hand,
On the back of my neck,
Like you used to do,
My Love.
Because Two Years,
Is Two Years,
Too Long.

UNEMPLOYED

I don't want to be held.

I want to hold.

That's what I do.

I built these biceps for you.

But you're dead.

And I'm unemployed.

MONOCLE

Hovel & Hobble

Skull & Bobble

The Thunder Woke The Dead.

So Downstairs I descend,

For a glass of water,

But I go for Milk instead,

As I'm already dead.

I check upon the Hell Hound,

Who said,

"Garble, growl, gravel, grovel, gargle."

Dog Noises.

Domesticated Wolf Noises.

Ruff Ruff

"It's The End!"

The Dog Said.

I tip the Top Hat,

Upon My Head,

"Right you are, Old Man!"

Now back to bed!

Up the stairs I glide,

Upon my side,

A Novel thing, I dare

Climbing a stair.

I extinguish the Light

With one tentacle.

I slide into my bed,

Constructed of femurs

Who were these Human Creatures,

Who once roamed this land?

I close my eye.

Nighty Night.

SUNFLOWER

I happened upon you,

Growing amongst the concrete

In the city, where the *YRR*

plant their churches.

Come with me my dear.

I'll take you away.

Far away,

From the movers and shakers.

Come with me to the edge,

Of the empire.

Come plant your roots with me,

Deep outside the camp.

Let's bloom in flyover country

Let's laugh at the influencers,

Who pity us.

Come, let us grow laugh lines,

And read Wendell Berry,

Out on the prairie.

HUSH

It's no joke.

I found the perfect Woman,

And ended up having to Shepherd

Her in Death,

Rather than Shepherd

Her in Life.

My Life.

Close your eyes sweetie.

Rest your head upon my chest.

My heart beats only for you.

Hush.

Shhh.

It's okay baby.

Shhh.

Soak my T-Shirt with your tears.

It's okay.

You done fought the good fight.

Curl up in my lap.

I built these arms for you.

Let my arms be your fortress.

Let me gently kiss your bald head.

You done well.

Honey.

Shhh.

It's alright.

It's time to go Home.

MORNING LIGHT

The Morning Light.
The Mourning Light.
Mourning Lite
What we look like
In Dawn's Early Light
When the Blood has drained
From our opinionated lips
In The Morning Light
In The Mourning Light
The People searched
Their hearts
The People yearned
To return to the Land
But the Land was Lost
In the Bloodshed.

"You know,

When I was a boy

All we ate was milk,

Peanut butter,

And BREAD."

The village Children

Look at the Geezer

Aghast.

"You & your tales, Grampy!"

They Scamper Off.

MRS. FRANKENSTEIN

She talked about the pain
Of ghosts & past memory
I said that was all good for me
As I ticked & drew her near
Foreboding & Fear

After all, did I not pull her

From A Dream?
Did she ever exist,
Apart from me?
I slapped her on the rump
With my bloody stump.
I don't discuss what I cannot amend.
Imma Man.
She's a Monster.

CRUCIFIED

The day

we married,

the Lord Crucified

my hand to yours.

I couldn't Leave

even If I wanted to.

I don't.

BLACK TRUCK

When you're gone
I'll drive that old black truck
around,
hating the world,
around the world,
because the world
builds monuments
to people who didn't matter,
never you.
I'll drive that old black truck
around, hating the world
like I drove that old black truck,
loving the world,
away from the Church
with you at my side,
White dress,
petite hand,
in mine.
I'll close the door of my heart
like I opened the door
of that old black truck

for you on our first date

and all the dates

and days

between

now and then,

then and eternity.

How long will I

automatically open

the passenger door

for a memory?

How Long, O Lord?

I see that old black truck

when I catch my gaze

in the mirror,

broke down,

rusting away

in the back alley,

cracked block,

broke heart,

time to go home.

THE FACIST

The world would be better
she said,
If all the men wore suits,
and all the lapels were
more pointed.

I SHOULD LIKE

I should like

to walk
without continuously getting snagged
on my rough edges.

I should like
to walk
amongst tall wind swept
prairie grasses,
swept off my feet,
stuck in your honey,
soft hands ministering
the balm of Gilead
to rough edges
and gapping wounds
which
tell my story,
footnotes and all.
Your soft hands
soften the story structure

before it collapses on my head,
yet again.

I should like
to walk,
forlorned wood
with you.

I should like
to wear
an old brown corduroy blazer
over & over,
'til people consider
my legendary eccentricities
legendary humility.

I should like
to work wood
like my grandfather,
'til the rough edges
wear smooth,
'til my hands wear rough,
like my old soul.

I should like

to preach behind the same

old wood pulpit

'til its rough edges,

as well as mine,

are worn smooth

by the Word.

I'm real monogamous like that.

I'd like to stand there

in a sawdusty brown corduroy blazer,

rough hand cupped in your softness,

'till you wear down my rough edges.

GARBAGE SANTA

What if Santa Claus
was a garbage man?
But instead of a sleigh,
he took our garbage away
in a big smelly truck
on Christmas day?

A day of atonement,
if you will,
when we awake,
giddy as children
to see our baggage
taken away?

We'd wrap our burdens
in tidy packages,
kicked to the curb,
just as we were,
tiny unspeakable burdens,
heavy beyond measure.

God bless you, Garbage Santa,

soggy stogie,

plumber's crack,

stained red satin suit,

getting your hands dirty

on the nightshift.

Christmas Eve,

time and a half.

Come first light,

we'd all run and smush

our snotty 'lil noses

against grimy windows,

bouncing like giddy children,

just to behold empty garbage cans,

carelessly strewn about the street.

THE LEMMINGS OF LOVE

Let's flap our wings
in the oil spill
of Love.

We'll be oblivious
to the world
and her cruel realities,
like an ostrich,
head stuck
in the forgetful sand
of Love.

We are the Lemmings of Love,
throwing ourselves headfirst over
the cliff
of Love.

I would,
for you.
For you,
I would.

And for none other
would I.

BUILD A NEW WING

Your heart was tender
toward mine in spring,
yes, even a bit of summertime
too,
'til you wanted access
to the dusty old rooms of my heart,
long boarded up
out of necessity.
You wanted what was
when all I could offer
was to build a new wing.

COMING SOON

The sign read

"Coming Soon,"

but soon never came.

They spent so much time

remodeling,

they forgot about the cawfee,

like that Macaulay Culkin movie

where he tells the pigeon lady

about his roller blades he loved so much

but never used.

Roll with me here.

I'd sit in a dump,

happy as a clam,

or even a lark.

I'd sit in a dump,

with a smile

if the cawfee was decent.

Perfection is no friend of mine.

THE SPINE OF THE WORLD

Down At The Base
Of The Spine Of The World
I Felt The Weight Of It All
Every Time I Reached
For The Small Of Her Back
And Felt Nothing
Except One More Day
Without Her.

ON THIS DAY

Let us go down to the River Styx

and quietly have our sins

and memories washed away.

Here, stand here

against this cabin wall.

Hold these sunflowers

with little purple things.

Hold them near.

Hold them dear.

Smile. This is the happiest day...

this picture won't hurt you a bit,

only me,

all the days from this one to that,

'til they bury me next to you.

Bury me with the picture

of her with the sunflower bouquet.

Bury me next to her

down by the tree line.

I'll hand it to her and say,

"Which is better? That day or this?

Surely we are younger yet Older.

Surely we are more Beautiful.

Surely we are more in Love.

Surely we are more Alive.

Surely we are more...

Than we were before

On This Day."

As We Rise.

HILARIUM

Your smile was a capsized vessel.

It sank in swirling waters,
deep in your mind,
beyond recovery,
sleeping with the fish.
Maybe joy will startle
you out of the past.
I'd like to court your chortle,
spending my days submerged
in my irreverent submarine,
dredging the bottom
of your broken heart
for that long-lost smile.
Nothing is beyond repair
if a laugh we share.
Maybe we'll put it together,
together,
so I can spend my days
cracking you up.
A boy could do worse

than spending his days

making a girl laugh.

I feel myself dying
A little bit more
Everyday.
The nights I spend
Pacing these halls.
My wicked little life
Ebbs and flows,
Too Slow,
To Help, or Stop,
To Save the date.
I can't make sense of it.
I mourn & mourn,
In the ash heap of history,
gardening.

In Ashes Thus,
Woe & Wooing
Lament & Tears,
Pure Horror,
Melody & Melancholia,
I grew utterly weary of darkness.

I said "Let us walk in the Light,

All the rest of our days.

Let us abide in Light."

The Empty House replied sweetly,

"Let's."

But the darkness consented not.

Night and Sleep flee from mine eyes.

It's already tomorrow.

5 a.m. is knocking.

The Dead are tending

To the new arrivals.

Misery Loves My Company,

As once did you, Honey.

Oh Rage.

Oh Blood curdling,

Bittersweet Rage.

I'd break everything in this house of mourning,

Were these things not of you.

OCTOBER OBITUARY

I lay my head
down to sleep,
down by the river
where the bones grow.

I will write
my October obituary
in the blood of Christ
while an old DJ
drives me to the Church
in a van without seats.

There I cried out
to God in silence:
"Remember me,
when you enter your kingdom."

the leaves fall
like my doubt
this is a new song
loud enough to fill the world

loud enough to shake the timbers of it all.

HGTV

Peeling paint,
pealing saint,
piddle & puddle,
pail & scuttle,
screechy, sketchy, kettle,
drip, drippity,
leaky roof,
what a pity.
I'll settle
down here
forever
'til you come home
to me.
Crank up the phonograph.
drown out the plucky neighbor.
They want to restore
my home
they call an "eyesore."
I cannot afford
the absurdity of it all.
Our Home, an eyesore?

Our eyes don't work the same.

I blow your daguerreotype a kiss.

Screaming kettle,

sounds like me

and my mettle.

TV producers skedaddle.

"Vintage." "Potential." "Character."

Prattle.

Chains rattle.

"Not For Sale!" I slam my fist

on the mantle.

You tease, "You dirty ghost, you."

I reply, "Better ghost than ghoul."

All they hear is "Boo."

We float,

you & I,

round and round,

in our nightly dance.

"Turn up the phonograph,"

I whisper in your ear,

"This is our Home.

We will never

leave our Home."

CHILI METAPHOR

I...
Like...
Your Chili.
You're spicy.
Familiar.
You keep these old bones warm.
If life's a cook-off,
I'm always on your side.
I'll award you the blue ribbon,
Each time.

Were I a cracker,
And Life broke me,
I should like to drown in you.

Were you a bowl of Chili...
I wouldn't mind...
Chili stains on my favorite shirt.
Just saying.
If this is a Chili Metaphor,
It isn't a Chilly Metaphor.

Whether you sustain or burn,

I like your Chili.

GLASSES

I still gaze

Through this old prescription,

Hoping to see the World

As I did when you were in it.

Life had been

One big raw deal.

So it came as a piss warm surprise

When he fell into the fire

After a long night of drinking

Black Velvet.

That not only did he not care

If he burned,

But that...he could not burn.

FIRST TIME FOR EVERYTHING

I remember waking up
And seeing you
For the first time.
We fell in love,
As if by design.
We fell in love,
As if there were
No one else in the world.
The world lay before us.
Nothing behind.
I reached for your hand
And said,
"If we would have met
1,000 years in the past
We still would have fell
Head over heels."
We both laughed.
There's only ever been now.

How Long Has It Been?
There's only ever been here.

There's only ever been you

And me, in the Garden of our Love.

There's only ever been this Love,

The greatest Love there's ever been,

Here in this Garden of our Love.

Everything we do we do anew.

I woke up and saw you

For the first time.

I named you Eve

He named me Man.

IF YOU RETURNED

If you returned to me
after all these years,
the same scientists who deny
resurrection
and true love
as more than chemical
would go incognito.
Neil deGrasse Tyson would shave his mustache,
muttering how we're all stardust
as he caught a greyhound bus.
Sioux City or bust.
Bill Nye's bow tie
would unfurl like bat wings
as he flew off into the night,
if you returned to me.

CARDIGAN

He gave the cardigan
To the Woman
Behind the Counter
With great care.
He gave her exact change,
But meant, "Never Change."

She placed the cardigan
Into the bag with great care.
Leaning over the counter,
She said, "Never machine wash,"
But meant, "Never Change."

THE TALKING HEADSTONES

That year it rained
so much,
all the solar flag lights
went dark.
The flag remains lit,
burning in my heart.
You've been gone
since 2014.
I hear time
passes differently there.
I hear the caretaker
takes all my cares
&
takes all my tears:
storing them in little bottles.
I hear Heaven ran out of bottles.
Sorry,
your hometown burned in a race riot.
Donald Trump is president.
I accidentally broke your favorite dish,
the one you made my favorite dish in:

shepherd's pie.

Will there be anything left of you

that doesn't reside in me?

I wonder what you'd say

about torch carrying

and stubbornness...

I reproach myself for not knowing.

If you came back today,

would you recognize the man

I am without you?

I can't find the answers in my books,

so I turned to writing them.

I'm lost in poems now.

I read in the paper

that Americans bought more poems last quarter.

Poems were up 2%.

However, less Americans chose to rent poems

while poem building plummeted.

ENTER THE DRAGON

Dragons breath fire,

not merely for terror,

not merely for roasting,

not merely for knight-slaying

(you'll thank me later, princess)

but because they have more Passion

than a mortal body can bear.

Because she flew off

and maybe, just maybe

if he incinerates enough villages,

she'll see the smoke signals.

The day the coffee stopped working,

we all had another cup

just to make sure.

We drank each cup down

to dystopian dregs,

and munched on the grounds.

Robert Frost lay in a stupor,

with all the paths diverging

before him, untraveled.

Hemingway is very much alive,

happily petting all the cats.

Unpublished: Dr. Claw.

Maybe next time he'll get it.

Forrest Gump became a couch potato,

trading shrimp for tater chips.

Stars Hallow burned under star fire.

#TEAMWOOKIE.

The day the coffee stopped working.

TO DANIELLE ON HER 33rd BIRTHDAY

I wasn't there.
But I'm sure
All the Sunflowers
Smiled the day you appeared
Resplendent in sorrow.
Resplendent in Resurrection.

You were innocent
Like the first bite
Of Birthday Cake,
Like all the Cotton Candy,
Ice cream camouflaged
In a torrent of sprinkles.

When you had the damned cancer
I bought you a piñata for your birthday.
And like a piñata
I could not bear
To watch you break.
Even though we both believed
In Him who said lest a grain of wheat

Fall into the Earth....

Upon cool Earth I lay,

Bouquet, Cake, Soggy Ice Cream Carton.

I read that electrical currents

Creep up and down

Tree roots

1/3 of an inch per second.

If I lay here long enough

Will they come

Pull me down to you?

I saw you teetering

Upon the precipice of Forever.

Life is a death march.

Let us march,

Hand in hand.

If you were rain

I'd want to drown

in a flood of you.

Reign over me,

Wave after Wave,

'til we melt into one,

Down by the River

Where sin & shame

Were washed away

By Resurrection Promises.

Pull me down

To the root of it all,

Deep down to the spine

Of the Earth.

Pull me down

And wash away

The Monsters

Who have built little Houses

Here & there

In my head.

Pull me down

And blow out these Candles.

For the burning is more

Than I can bear.

For unless a grain of wheat

Falls into the Earth

And Dies

It remains alone

But if it dies...

I'LL SHOW ME YOURS IF YOU SHOW ME MINE

Show Me All Your Dead.

Show Me All The

Haunts & Hallows,

Holy Places,

And Holiday Scenes

That Could Be.

Breathe Life Into Me.

Show Me The Haunts & Hallows

In Your Head.

Or Instead,

You And I

Could Go

On Adventures.

We Could Build

A Kingdom Out Of The Skulls

Of What Could've Been

And What Should've Been

And ALL That Was,

All Our Favorites.

We Could Weave A Rope

Out Of The Doubt Snake

Coiled In The Pit Of Our Stomachs,

Tempered Fortitude,

Soft Winter Cheek Kisses,

Sitting On The Dock.

I'll Still Be Here

When Walls Fall.

SUNDAY

I have noticed
A precipitous
Drop in emails
On Sunday.
Somehow,
This give me Hope
For Mankind
After All.

He winked at her

But meant,

"Ring The Church Bell.

Kiss me

In the noonday Sun,

Bright & Hot.

Kiss them laugh lines,

Those Long Lost Friends Of Mine,

Returned to this world weary face

Like the prodigal son,

When you embraced me from far off.

Let us nod and smile,

Wink and Weather

The Storm,

The People,

With their opinions,

tantrums, and preferences,

'til we find shelter

Home Alone."

OLD FRANK

Old Frank

Is an itchy eared

Mutt of suspect heritage.

His rap sheet is gnawed upon,

replete with rapt denials.

Dogs know repentance,

But save it for the Master.

Frank keeps no record of wrongs,

But he weighs a dog pound

In the dog days of summer,

calculated in dog years.

On those Days I believe he's immortal.

I believe my own lies.

He's just

An itchy eared mutt, after all.

He shakes his head with piss and vinegar

When I pour medicinal powder

Into his itchy ears.

He shakes until he's dancing

And prancing

In a cloud of white.

I suspect he'd rather

Have his ears scratched

Than healed.

We're the same like that.

I am allergic to dogs,

But far more allergic am I

To a life without my friend.

Old Frank knows

I would have been happy enough

In old run-down Waterloo,

Fishing and working

On Old cars with Dad.

Maybe he'd let slip,

The secret to life,

Between the rhythm and beats

Of turning Wrenches and Worlds.

I'd be happy in old Waterloo,

where the yuppies

Make sure you know they live in Cedar Falls.

But a man goes where a man will,

To find work here and there,

And Home is wherever Old Frank

Snores at my feet.

Bald head & cataracts.

We sit in the diner,

The noisy one by the interstate.

"My eyes water,"

he explains by way of apology,

"don't much matter what I do.

I should go to the doctor,

but doctors!

Who needs that?

know what I mean?"

He sighs as he crumples his napkin,

staring off into space.

As cars fly by,

he muses that when he meets Jesus,

he'll have enough tears to wash His feet,

but not enough hair to dry them.

He wonders if he's the last believer

as a droid clears the table,

as the man clears his throat,

and tries to swallow the lump

and hold back the tears,

'til the day he meets Him.

WHERE NO ONE KNOWS YOUR NAME

The Father

Sprawls on his back,

Down & out.

His head isn't in the sand,

But noise canceling headphones

Halo his head.

An empty bottle of Fireball

Graces his hand.

In the hay loft, he makes his bed

Through cracks & holes.

In shelter, he spies

Wrens,

Blue Birds

&

Gold Finches.

Swimming in music,

Drowning his sorrow in poetry,

He takes a trip back to stuffy, heady days

Before optimism was snuffled,

Before his will shuffled.

They'd talk about having kids,

Which was really jumping the gun

Or perhaps the shark,

Whatever that means,

While laying on empty crumbling

Bleachers.

Two, broken by pain,

Wondered if they could make family again

Out of fragile fragments

Held together by bailing wire & religion.

When I was an Atheist,

I was pretty & sure

Christians put steeples on Churches

To amplify their prayers so loud,

Even their slumbering God could hear them.

Now I know they are meant to remind

Mortal man that we have but

the breath of life in our nostrils.

And of what account are we any who?

Prayers that is.

Steeples too.

So I know Wendell Berry's "That Distant Land"

Is Perfect,

But 100 years in Port William

Probably should have included a few more Preachers.

No Worries.

Marilynne Robinson gave us Gilead, Iowa.

BOOK LOVERS

Let us Go to Narnia

Where it's always Winter

And never Christmas

And there's nothing to do

But...

Stay inside.

You. Are.

My Favorite Book.

I wanna read you all over

And memorize every

Dog-eared page.

You think your binding is broken

But I'm gunna hold you

By the spine.

So take off your dust cover, girl.

You ain't gunna need it.

Because you know

I won't leave you

On the Shelf.

A QUESTION

How Can the Honeymoon

Be over?

When you

Are My Honey

And Moon

And the Stars reigning high overhead,

The Trees stretching their branches

To Heaven while anchoring the world

With your roots, all the while making the air

My children will breathe in, only to exhale "Mama!"?

How...

Did you get so beautiful?

And How...

Did you find the strength to dare,

And the strength to stand

tall against the naked sky

and prying eyes,

quizzical glances of the passersby?

All the while defying the gravity of it all,

providing the shade

In which you have healed all the wounds death
inflicted

The day he cornered me and demanded I flinch and
cower,

Kneel and bow before him forever?

Because you are life and Love

And all things kind and shimmering

On the edge of the magic,

Living right in front of my face.

Yet I do not have to believe,

Because you are everywhere I look.

The final frontier.

I catch glimpses,

Here and there,

Of Future Days we share,

Out of the corner of my eye.

My peripheral vision

And Gut

Don't lie.

They tell me, "Settle Down Boy,

Don't be scared of a good thing.

Don't be one of those people

Who are too stupid to let themselves be Happy."

Let our blue eyes meet.

I am the Pacific Ocean

And All My Life I Ain't Been Nobody But Me,

And wave upon wave will tell you,

"I ain't scared.

I ain't scared one bit."

Death said he'd return for me

And I'm sure he will,

But he's the only one who can tear me away from you.

And I ain't scared,

I ain't scared a'tall.

Acknowledgments

Rachel Welcher made this happen. Boys, get yourself a wife who believes in you. Never let her go. Especially during the dark watches of the night. I Love You, Rach.

Evan Welcher is the senior pastor of Vine Street Bible Church in Glenwood, Iowa. After losing his wife to cancer, Evan wrote the book *Resplendent Bride*, chronicling the love and loss of his first marriage. He now lives with his wife, Rachel, and their dog, Frank, in a house on a hill.

Made in the USA
Coppell, TX
26 June 2021